FOR THE BODY

FOR
THE BODY

Poems by Marilyn Nelson Waniek

Louisiana State University Press
Baton Rouge and London

1978

Copyright © 1978 by Marilyn Nelson Waniek
All rights reserved
Manufactured in the United States of America

Design: Patricia Douglas Crowder
Typeface: VIP Trump Medieval
Composition: Graphic Composition, Inc., Athens, Georgia
Printer and Binder: Thomson-Shore, Inc.

"I Imagine Driving Across Country" and "My Grandfather Walks in
the Woods" originally appeared in *Hudson Review;* "The Life of a
Saint" appeared in *Carleton Miscellany.*
Other poems in this volume originally appeared in *Motley, Con-
crete Statement,* and *Georgia Review.*

LIBRARY OF CONGRESS CATALOGING IN PUBLICATION DATA

Waniek, Marilyn Nelson, 1946–
 For the body.

 I. Title.
PS3573.A4795F6   811'.5'4   78–18442
ISBN 0–8071–0463–9
ISBN 0–8071–0464–7 pbk.

For my people: you know who you are.

CONTENTS

The Language We Speak Is Not the One We Dream

FOR THE BODY

DEDICATION

For the heart
in its stone boat
that falls always
through this clear,
this black water.
For the heart,
the most desperate organ.
The heart, bailing us out.

For the brain,
the center of miracles,
with its dreams of flying
over the woods and meadows,
the body hanging by its beard.
For the brain, the maker,
its tiny star light.

And for the hands,
for all the working class
of the body: feet, belly, legs.
For all the other unsung
we have no nice names for.
For our proletariat,
our common man.

For all the body
whose messages we do not heed.
For the body,
riding its pain and pleasure.
For the body,
living like a beacon
out into death.

DRIVING HOME

MY GRANDFATHER
WALKS IN THE WOODS

Somewhere
in the light above the womb,
black trees
and white trees
populate a world.

It is a March landscape,
the only birds around are small
and black.
What do they eat,
sitting in the birches
like warnings?

The branches of the trees
are black and white.
Their race is winter.
They thrive in cold.

There is my grandfather
walking among the trees.
He does not notice
his fingers are cold.
His black felt hat
covers his eyes.

He is knocking on each tree,
listening to their voices
as they answer slowly
deep, deep from their roots.
I am John, he says,
are you my father?

They answer
with voices like wind
blowing away from him.

MAMA
I REMEMBER

Mama I remember.
My hair was in braids—
you tapped done with the comb
and I stood up between your knees.
You were always
packing for the movers,
sitting in front of me
when I touched my father's hair.
You never cried,
wrapped glasses in newspaper,
took the pictures down.
The last baby grew
warped in your womb,
smiled three years
and died. I remember
your eyes when you climbed
into the ambulance.
You patted my cheek,
your hands wet with blood.

You stared
when I slapped the wall
and cursed the hospital
where my father died.
Now you meditate.
I understand
your need, the soft ache
of loss in your thighs.

I am you again
as you walk through the corridor.
The ceiling is as high as heaven
and echoes your tapping feet on the waxed floor.
Nobody stares at you yet,
a small black child too awkward to play ball.

You stop at Mrs. Purdy's door.
It opens.
Five rows of blue and green eyes
like the marbles you won last summer
that you keep in the old fish bowl.
Five times six faces
under hair like straw, like silk,
like the mule's tail
if the mule's tail were table brown
or dry grass brown
or brown as orange pop with coke.

The faces like empty sheets of pale paper
watching you,
waiting to see you jig
or wet your pants
or marry someone's sister.

You go in
and I go with you.
We sit all year alone
on one side of the room
and learn only years later
how loudly we can say our names.

MRS. HONG'S
HOUSE

In joy
I enter sleep
and Mrs. Hong's house,
a castle of dark rooms
smelling of moss and antiques.
I push aside curtains,
allow the air to enter,
make the heavy green scent
move like deep water
over pictures of ancestors
lined on the mantel
and the dark rooms
of doily-covered chairs.
I wake with
an egg of joy
growing under my ribs.
In it, a faceless pool
with no reflections,
full of little fish.

Their feathers
their feathers were like white silk
and their bodies black
against the pale sky.

The girls and their parents
used to live on the next block.
I've nodded to them often in passing.
But strange.
The girls with their books,
never played with dolls
the way you'd expect.
And no boyfriends.
The mother seemed
to live in a dream.
And the father.
I remember his talk—
"I think I'll fly."
Of course we never put
much stock in that.
A funny sort of people,
but decent neighbors.

The rise was strenuous.
Those bodies lifted by the arms
not made to lift,
the puny shoulders
a forest of feathers,
the strained face of the woman,
the man's mouth tight,
their eyes squeezed barely open.
And the girls nervous,
young bodies tensed
to the touch of sky.

This.
This touch.
Mother and daughters,
a dark aging man,
their feathers.
Their feathers were like white silk.

I DECIDE
NOT TO HAVE CHILDREN

Dawn, the gulls weep for the Jews,
and up through my muddy blood
my lost sister rises like a drowned puppy.
I'd forgotten how far away
I'd sent her, wonder how it was
in that wet country,
her skin melting back into mine.
There were nights
I almost recognized her face,
like an old rose pressed under glass.
Sometimes she made
a knock in the pipes
faint as a heartbeat
and backed away again.

In some small room of myself
she has shrunk
to the size of a sparrow
since the night the soldiers came
and searched through my dreams
in their angry uniforms.
I find her there, halfway to sleep,
a sister smaller than a hare
in the blind appendix
behind my eyes.

I'd forgotten how much I cared
and she comes holding out
her fat brown fists,
the flowers of mourning
already twisted in her hair.
Her faint body makes a light
that warms the whole house.

THE AMERICAN
DREAM

I want to go shopping
and buy myself.
I want to suddenly turn
american, sold at the counter
by some sleight-of-mind
salesman who'll trap my dreams
and put me in an automatic cage.

I want my face to stop looking
like an african housewife,
my feet to stop dancing to
lost music.

I want to get out of
my VW some saturday afternoon
and walk through silent glass doors.
I want to pick myself up
in Safeway.

We're old war-horses,
you and I.
The kind the Indian said
was too embarrassed to retreat.
The kind with scars
that made even the enemy sorry,
with manes eaten by the wind.
We'll be an old soldier's memory
by an open fire in his garden
twenty years from now.
It's uncanny, he'll say
near tears, she saved my life.

I dreamed this.
Yet you're my human sister.
I come to you now
with a conscience that's grown
bigger than my heart,
my tongue burning
with true poems to tell you.

We're old war-horses, Jennifer.
But when I step back from you
and see your shadow
like a tongue of black fire
spreading from your toes
I see more than your real skin.
I see something wonderful,
the shadow of a horn.

I neither remember
the first time
nor the last.

Only once
another child
in a pink dress
stood on her father's lawn
barefooted,
her eyes hard with laughter
as I walked by.

I remember
a first day at school.
Someone met me on the playground,
smiled with me
past teeter-totters
bobbing like oil derricks
and the slide shining gold
in the sun.
That time
a sixth-grader
looked our way,
aimed his eyes carefully,
and shot me with
america.

THE FISH
WEEPS

The fish weeps
in her bed every night.
She wants to have breasts.
She wants to have blond hair
with sunlight on it.
She wants to be kissed
by the man in the movies,
her fish heart to pound stars.
The fish isn't happy
being the fish.
She wants strong legs
with a penis between them.
She wants to hold the line
with the hook on the end.
She wants to have brown skin
and crisp hair.
She wants to teach school every day.
She wants my eyes.
She wants my husband,
the sound of my voice.
She wants an ass.
She wants you to be reading
the poem I am writing about her
but she wants to write it.
She weeps every night
wanting to be me.

OTHER WOMEN'S CHILDREN

In Wyoming,
plain as far as my eye can see,
there are towns behind mountains,
towns beyond rivers, at the edge
of the range, across peaks
I will never climb.

Driving,
I think constantly
of other women's husbands.
Their sleek bodies,
their smiles,
the pressure of their hands
on my back dancing.

In these towns the husbands tend
lawns polished to jade luster.
The houses bloom
like muted flowers, the kitchens
are neat as pins.

I think of the quiet lives
under the elm trees
of every small town
in the midwest.
The bright housedresses.
The clean children
with smooth white knees,
the children who never cry.

CHURCHGOING
after Philip Larkin

The Lutherans sit stolidly in rows;
only their children feel the holy ghost
that makes them jerk and bobble and almost
destroys the pious atmosphere for those
whose reverence bows their backs as if in work.
The congregation sits, or stands to sing,
or chants the dusty creeds automaton.
Their voices drone like engines, on and on,
and they remain untouched by everything:
confession, praise, or likewise, giving thanks.
The organ that they saved years to afford
repeats the Sunday rhythms song by song;
slow lips recite the credo, smother yawns,
and ask forgiveness for being so bored.

I, too, am wavering on the edge of sleep,
and ask myself again why I have come
to probe the ruins of this dying cult.
I come bearing the cancer of my doubt
as superstitious suffering women come
to touch the magic hem of a saint's robe.

Yet this has served two centuries of men
as more than superstitious cant; they died
believing simply. Women, satisfied
that this was truth, were racked and burned with them
for empty words we moderns merely chant.

We sing a spiritual as the last song,
and we are moved by a peculiar grace
that settles a new aura on the place.
This simple melody, though sung all wrong,
captures exactly what I think is faith.
Were you there when they crucified my Lord?
That slaves should suffer in his agony!
That Christian, slave-owning hypocrisy
nevertheless was by these slaves ignored

as they pitied the poor body of Christ!
Oh, sometimes it causes me to tremble,
that they believe most, who so much have lost.
To be a Christian, one must bear a cross.
I think belief is given to the simple
as recompense for what they do not know.

I sit alone, tormented in my heart
by fighting angels, one group black, one white.
The victory is uncertain, but tonight
I'll lie awake again, and try to start
finding the black way back to what we've lost.

I imagine driving across country
with my sister and brother.
In California we buy caps,
the kind truck drivers wear,
bright colors that keep the sun away.
We take turns at the wheel
and sing all the songs we know.
My sister's voice is like mine
and I stop singing to listen.
All night we drive through the mountains.

My brother pulls the car over
at noon in the desert
and we get out to stretch our legs.
A strange man takes our picture
standing beside the car
in our decorative skins.

In the car again
we make the other trips,
through Kansas and Oklahoma
in the pink Lincoln and the Kaiser.
We count Uncle Sam mailboxes
and white horses,
we sleep at dusk-to-dawn drive-ins.

I catch the beautiful slow smile
of our dead brother
in the rearview mirror,
and our father in his uniform
drives 80 and when the cop stops us
—What do you think you're flying, boy?—
he answers: B-52's.

Now we are telling jokes in the farmland,
playing the dozens, getting down.

In Maine we get out to see the ocean.
We have come home again,
our old house there on the hill.

That night none of us can sleep.
In our separate rooms we lie awake
in the shared darkness
and imagine ourselves
still driving across country,
still falling home down the highway.

THE ICE CREAM WOMAN

After the first week
I stopped
dreaming potatoes
chocolate ice cream
macaroni and cheese.
Everything was easier.
I cleaned out the kitchen,
put nonperishables
into clean well-sealed jars.

One night there was
a child in my dream.
She had no hands.
I rocked her,
taught her to count.
This, I thought,
is interesting.

Every morning I weigh myself,
I measure my skin.
This diet is wonderful.
I can eat myself all up.
I will go all the way.
My brain will gnaw the bones,
everything must go.
The brain will eat itself,
leave nothing at all
but a sad little residue
of hunger.

APRIL
RAPE

Bessie Altmann is home again,
locked in so tight she can't take a breath,
the mouths of all the locks in the house
snatch at her air like cats.

But she wants it this way.
She likes the house tight as a skin
corset around her waist,
no breeze to wrap fingers there
and whisper like he did
please please please.

Bessie Altmann avoids mirrors,
dark eyes that look into hers:
Let me go.

It is April in Philadelphia,
in her two rooms she breathes
and breathes again her body's smell.
She wants to hide in a book,
small enough to slip unnoticed
between the lines of black print
and never be seen again.

She considers alternatives:
A knife. A razor blade tucked
neatly between lip and gum.
Karate. Mace. A gun.
But she knows these will never work.

She is trying to grow teeth everywhere.
She will bite the next man that comes,
eat him up like a piece of ice.
She is glad to be home again.

VENEZUELA:
THREE PLACES

I. *Margarita*

Ay,
these slender women
spread their nakedness
on the sand
as coolly as they drape
laundry to dry.

Drive through
any pueblo
and you'll see them
hanging on hedges,
smoothed across
the grassy spot
in front of the door.

II. *Coro*

If I lived here
my world would be
reduced
to grunts.
It's too damn hot.
Everything conspires
to hold me down.
Here one day,
already I'm a
fat squat
in the doorway.

III. *Merida*

A paw or two
begs for popcorn,
other animals
unrecognizable
turn to the wall
away from you.

The water buffalo
cries real tears
while you watch,
and a heavy mist
stinking of urine
hangs over the zoo.

Señor
nosotros somos pobres,
we are poor

The children pursue you
blue-eyed in ponchos
down the Andes
through the valleys,
all the way home.

THE ICE CREAM
WOMAN

You are kind,
but there is something missing.
She was not always good,
this quiet and pale,
hands folded.
A madwoman sometimes,
she taught us the value
of silence.
We built castles in the dust
under every bed in the place
hiding from her angry hands;
I remember how she danced
one morning by the telephone
when she hung up on the priest.

Mother, mother,
they have measured your mouth.
They have smoothed down your hair,
made your eyes close decently.
But you were a yellow lion,
and your rage would burst
and spatter its bitter milk over us
if you could see how we have made you
the ice cream woman,
how we stroke tenderly
your still and painted face.

A DEAF
OLD LADY

Voices have darkened
to a gray peace,
and in silence,
her private room
in the old folks
welfare ward,
she listens for movement
with her slowing eyes.

There are no flights
of birds,
no children
screaming through
the walls,
no bursts of anger
from the street
to wake her.
Only her wild old hair
frenzies around her face.

At night
she lies black
in the stippled darkness
and dreams that she has fallen
without taking leave
toward this small end
the whole of her life.

WOLF
WHEEL

I twirl moons
on my birth
control wheel
till the last one
is darkened
and a new moon rises
like hackles
on the back
of my neck.
I snarl
at breakfast,
prowl like a
cop car
around the house.
My skin
buries itself
under heavy hair,
my hands claw,
my mouth
is suddenly
full of teeth.
I am out for blood,
a wolf with narrow eyes
howling.

I am the woman
against the moon
with the face of a rabbit
caught by both legs
in a narrow snare.

FRAU W,
FRAU J, FRAU E

I can imagine you
any way but dead.
Old girls, your age
surprised you, too:
somebody else's gray hairs,
somebody else's wrinkles
around your eyes.

I see you in the forties.
The air beats like mad bats
around your heads.
My friends are fists,
curled snails you do not own yet,
hearts that only whisper
the old insistent "I want."

All that decade men
carried their flags
like screams on the ends of sticks,
and you went down
into birth like lead,
each pain a mouth
with its own language.
My friends were strangers
behind a door,
hands at the other end
of the ropes you paid out
into a world you would never reach.

Now you have tied them
to your darkness
like patients
on the shock treatment table
while you rise triumphant
as great whales
into the light
on the surface of the water.

CANCER
ROSES

And Mary we are gardeners,
each growing frost roses
like dark lace
in our skins.

We will be successful.
We will be wrapped
in finish line ribbons.
The world will lean over us
to envy the unveiling
of our lives,
the gardens we have grown
in our anxiety.

We talk for hours.
We worry.
We cry, and smoke goes in
to feed flowers that bloom
like caviar
in our red flesh.

We are special, Mary.
We are thunder eggs.
They will break us open
to the sun
and find us different.

They will find black roses
spreading fingers
like crystal,
all the roses we grew
toward this change.

TWIST
THE THREAD

Twist the thread
three times around your finger.
Pull it through.
It's so easy you forget
day winding into evening.

Spring again.
The same birds whistle
their sweet marriages,
the same trees
weave out loops
of the same new green.

End of the row.
Go back.
Begin again the rosary of yarn.

It's so easy you forget,
knitting toward night,
and you correct your life.
You think of answers
you never gave,
remember the impossible,
the failures all success.
Your fingers, touching everyone,
have learned gentleness by heart.

The friends who died come back,
their faces red
with things to tell you.
And this time you listen
with wide eyes.

No longer alone in your language
of unanswered questions,
you knit the children right,

the love true,
the husband coming back.
Each stitch is true,
the thread taut,
the life complete in recollection,
the perfected past.

FOR MARY,
FOURTH MONTH

Open the drawer.
There are scissors there
like teeth in the darkness.
And, like a root,
someone is biting into
your darkness.

In your secrecy, so deep
you cannot think it out,
someone is opening hands.
O, slow and dark there,
someone is making room for hands.
Someone's legs are learning to beat
a tattoo you will not forget.
There is burrowing there,
a red light growing on the horizon,
a dim knock on your mind's door.

You shake your head.
Scissors, you say, like knives
are waiting for someone like me.
I am green, you say,
have forgotten the urgent pushings
of roots.
In the room of your body
someone is opening hands.
Someone is stretching, is dancing
to wet, secret music.
The beat, the beat of someone's feet
is teaching you new rhythms.

You awake with a start
as someone opens
sad, knowing eyes.

THE WRITER'S
WIFE

She watched him take his books away
into the bedroom,
where he stayed for hours on end.
She counted pencils whittled down
to nubs, their shiny leads
licked and rounded.
After suppers, as she drew
the dishes toward her
on the table, scraping bits
of fat and cold potato onto
her plate for the cat,
she bit her lip, watching him
rise to the newspaper.
She wanted a child.
Night after night, she lay
curled like a dog around her
womb, while he pecked away
at the typewriter in the other room.
When he published, she smiled
for the camera, licked
her thin lips
and turned away.

THE DREAM
LOVER

You close your eyes
and clamber down the blue stairway
toward sleep.
With every step
you grow smaller:
you are yourself again,
you clutch a one-eyed doll.

He appears as always
from back of the drapes.
He wraps long arms around you,
tickles and pinches,
leaves ecstatic bruises
that have never stopped saying his name.

This is the prince
with the magic kiss,
the mouth you tasted
in the first prim kiss that opened.
His eyes see you
and know you, grown up
and unchanged.

Coming all hot from your business,
made with the children
or drowsy after love,
you slow down to greet
a face that is tender,
a mouth that is silent and black.
He's the one you can't lose,
like your father;
your dream lover,
the harder counterpart
of who you think you are.

FOR
WANDA S.

Wanda, half the girls in Minneapolis
are dressing like you this spring.
Your blue jeans,
your light curly hair.
You are a fashion.
Strange to remember how "out" you were
ten years ago.

I meet your lily face
on all kinds of bodies,
only your low voice that never laughed
is missing.
And the eyes are other,
the mouths thin and smiling.

Wanda, when you said goodbye
in that deep quiet voice
again and again,
leaving for Europe,
Mexico, Pakistan,
you left a challenge like a glove
I never picked up.

I thought of you today
as I stared at your hair
on another girl,
and tears jumped into my eyes.
They are your lovers,
your children,
your friends,
the days we spent together
ten years younger,
the things we could have known
about each other
had I been braver
and you less brave.

ATLANTIC
IMMIGRATION

They leave their mothers,
step out like words
spoken for the first time.

They are somehow
beautiful,
they offer the future
on the silver platters
of their bodies.

You are my chosen people,
they said once,
I forsake myself to you.
Thy people shall be my people.
Never dreaming a brick and concrete
continent.

Brought up on love and duty
the daughters of Europe
listen now like Ruth
to the babble around them.
The infants they carry
in baskets, arms, in wombs
will not remember them,
will say bitterly,
My mother was old.

In the cold spray
around the stone woman's feet
they dream of wealth and freedom
and remember the warmth
of the circle around their mother's hearths.

And, yet in the bustling harbor,
as they turn to the men,
they see their lives
like clipper ships
disappear in the whirlpools
of the eyes of hope.

SILVER
EARRINGS

And so you walked
through the swinging door
of the third-floor ladies room
in Dayton's department store
on a Saturday afternoon
with great plans in mind.

(In mind a chart with pins on it,
the general announces
"we shall take this face."
He points to the whole map.
This is war.)

The silver earrings you put on
explode the quiet light
in your face.
You are the child again
who discovers in the room
marked *Girls*
the stain that makes her
a woman,
and walks back through the door
with a light in her eyes
part joy,
part fear.

FOR
KAREN

You are driving
through a landscape of catastrophes.
Cows in a field explode,
leave party streamers of meat
all over the grass.
Airplanes die on their backs
bleeding faces through their windows.
Fuel trickles quietly onto the road
and runs away in the ditch,
blood and gasoline
rainbow the pavement.
The car you were riding in
turns to light,
glass sings, falling
into your screams.

And now, Karen,
as the bits of glass
slice to the surface of your face
and come out again like memories,
you know you will never escape.
Fear surrounds you,
breathes its vapor heavy as love.

And you think
If I move
I may make a spark
and ignite the whole world.
I will never live again.

EMILY DICKINSON'S DEFUNCT

She used to
pack poems
in her hip pocket.
Under all the
gray old lady
clothes she was
dressed for action.
She had hair,
imagine,
in certain places, and
believe me
she smelled human
on a hot summer day.
Stalking snakes
or counting
the thousand motes
in sunlight
she walked just
like an Indian.
She was New England's
favorite daughter,
she could pray
like the devil.
She was a
two-fisted woman,
this babe.
All the flies
just stood around
and buzzed
when she died.

*THE LANGUAGE WE SPEAK
IS NOT THE ONE WE DREAM*

The language we speak
is not the one we dream.
Outside the tidy categories of man
the mind speaks slowly
in a language deeper than the tongue.
It speaks memory, with echoes of forgotten rooms,
desire licking moist lips,
hunger's bright alarm
and the red siren of fear
loosening white lights in the flesh.

The dog dreams
as it mutters there in the corner.
Something like a clap,
and through the synapses
goes the only thing the body knows as prayer.
And the dog dreams rabbits,
a quick bark among the trees.

The dog is dreaming a world,
the circles made as somewhere a loon
disappears into the dark lake.
The dog dreams smoke drifting past a tent,
a lean boy stringing his bow.
The dog dreams buffalo,
pale men like strange angels
driving the doomed down the ladder to death.

And the loon dreams head under wing
through the chilly night.
It dreams it has broken the barrier
between sound and speech.
The loon dreams it is human now;
it can recognize music.
In its dream it finds words
and wakes up creation: the world
grows big inside its mouth.

The loon is bursting with meaning;
it dreams me then, and dreams on.

Last night the dolphin came to me again,
all splendid in its huge wisdom.
I dreamed its voice came thin as water
out of the vague sea, and bloomed like dawn
over the chaos of sleep.

SICK
TOGETHER

For the first time
in our marriage
we were sick together
five gray days last week.

We lay in bed suffering,
twin invalids
comparing pains.
Are you cold too,
you gurgled through your nose,
and I hawked yes.
We pulled the blankets closer.

Three times a day
we gargled warm salt water,
our eyes meeting
in the bathroom mirror.
And we sipped soup,
drank hot lemon and honey,
ran through two boxes of kleenex
and a whole bottle of aspirin.

Later, we
could read between coughs,
talked about
how mothers used to nurse us
through dreamy sick afternoons,
making all medicine sweet.

This week we are well
and separate again.
The seal is broken.
We are no longer
one flesh
moving toward health,
toward death.

OLD
BIBLES

I throw things away
usually, but there's
this whole shelf
of Bibles in my house.
Old Bibles, with pages missing
or scribbled by children
and black covers chewed by puppies.
I believe in euthanasia,
but I can't get rid of them.
It's a sin,
like stepping on a crack
or not crossing your fingers
or dropping the flag.

I did that once,
and for weeks
a gaunt bearded stranger
in tricolored clothes
came to get me,
moaning,
Give me my flag.
And Bibles are worse,
they maybe have souls
like little birds fluttering
over the dump
when the wind blows their pages.
Bibles are holy, blessed,
they're like
kosher.

So I keep them,
a row of solemn apostles
doomed to life,
and I wait for the great collection
and conflagration,

when they'll all burn together
with a sound like the wings
of a flock of doves:
little ash ascensions
of the Word.

WHERE THE MONARCHS GO
for Pam

I'll go away with you
if there's a place.
We'll slip away
as quietly as winter
leaves the numb lakes.
We won't smile
like drawn bows or answer
desires imperative as clocks.
We'll go where the air chimes
around pine trees.

There's a simpler way to be
than the top of the hours
where the bells niagara down.
We can do better than this two-bit motel.
We won't pump iron with the poets
by the pool.

We'll find the way we lost
when we got nearsighted.
We'll leap like salmon
up the stream of light.
We'll go where the monarchs go,
or to Falcon Mountain,
where the air is cold and thin,
where hawks make gestures in the sky,
slow as smoke.

The gloved poet refuses
to dance with women.
Women, he says, bore him;
they have their own quiet uses
and he has his.
The gloved poet grows hair,
settles down into loneliness,
fills his own
small spaces.

THE LIFE
OF A SAINT

I. *The Saint Leaves His Father's House*

A boy walks out
onto the sun's bright stage.
The leaves are celebrating
the resurrection of birds,
the sky shouts hallelujah.
Nothing is more real than the dust
and the cobbled streets that shine
like water under his feet.
He is off to seek his fortune,
God, in the changing faces of the year.

A saint laughs
from the boy's throat;
his father's house becomes
a small reflection in his eyes.

II. *The Saint's Dream*

The saint gets up
in his skinny clothes.
His cave is cold and damp
as an April morning.
Even the sparrows
have found someplace to be warm.
The saint shivers to work:
he is performing penance for his eyes,
beheading all the flowers
that offend his sight.
He awakens suddenly on his feet
with his fists full of petals
and remembers his dazzling dream
of the night before.

He had entered the musical air
of the kingdom of heaven,
bared his head to the light

from five great thrones.
One throne,
fat cushions done in gold,
stood on a pedestal.

On the mountain
are only the wind
and the saint
but he hears
from the dust
like the voice of his mother,
long years dead,
someone saying,
"This was the chair of one
who would be holier than I."

III. *Seducing the Saint*

He was so pure
he only ate white flowers.
Nobody knew what his body
smelled like. His lips
opened and closed around prayers,
his thin skin was a bag
for blood and bones and a heart
that sang, beating,
the glory of God.

I went to him once
on a morning heavy with rain
to ask why my man
was a stranger to me
and why my womb worried
itself over and over to death
and hardly had knelt
at his punctured feet
when the dove of the Lord

entered my belly
and opened its trembling wings.

It was a revelation.
Fire leapt like dogs
from my hair,
my mouth came alive,
I could read the secrets
in the scent of his robe,
birds tingled in my fingers,
I felt the shadows melt back
in my eyes.

Folding his hands
into his sleeves,
the saint arose.
"The way of woman
leads to darkness,"
he said, and threw himself
into that thicket there.
But the roses knew me
and drew in their thorns.
Their leaves caressed him
in my name, buds burst
into ecstatic blossom
all around him.

IV. *The Saint Preaches*

The saint has come back to town.
Everyone comes out.
His father's old retainers
whisper how he's changed.
He says he has a mistress now,
that his pride kisses the ground.
He seems so strange.
He carries his hunger
in a wooden bowl.

Some say they see his mistress,
that she's old
and wears rags. He says
he's been praying for years.
When he limps
through the streets
he leaves red footprints
for the rain to eat.
He looks as wild as the baptist,
everyone says, but they hang around
anyway when he starts to preach.

He's talking to something beyond them,
it seems, no, something so close
they'd forgotten to notice,
like their own good stink
or the beauty of kitchens.
When he opens his arms they think
birds fly out like coins.
He speaks a language they understand
but can't speak.
It sounds to them like singing,
like the melody of the wind
in the gray olive trees.

They hang around all day
and when they go home
it seems better,
as if they'd discovered salt.
They forget the dark
they're afraid of
and remember all night long
how the saint opened his wings
among the gathering birds,
how he opened his beak,
how he sang.

THE
TOWER

Belief
is only the first step.
A seed, full of clasped hands,
will open in earth's muddy mouth
and push like a syllable out,
trusting its root to find moisture,
its pale leaf light.

You have seen
a heavy door swing open
in the deep vault of the sky.
Believe the light bulb's sway there
like a bright bell
and the answers in God's handwriting
you have found in the neat files.
But this is only the first step.

Next is a tower here on earth
drawn by a madman's hands
and filled with a dank odor
you know as your own.
By a trick of perspective
all directions are reversed;
there are no answers
but death's certitude;
no justice
but love's aging fingers;
no heaven
but a kingdom of stone.

Here despair will teach you
the language of praise,
to trust in nothing
but your humility,
your doubt.

GOOD NIGHT,
MRS. CALABASH

Right now is nowhere
to make a stand.
The last quarter
of the twentieth century,
the dishes are teeth
chattering on the shelf.
We'll grab on to anything
in this jello landscape,
hole up together with our enemies
in this year of vampires.

Let's face it, the war is over.
Our indignation's been pulled
right out from under our feet.
We can still laugh
in the teeth of love
but there is no mathematics
to count our losses.

Standing behind us in the mirror
is a child who knows it will never die.
But we will.
We stand with Mrs. Calabash and watch
the trees tilt into the horizon.
We'll learn to love this new territory.
Look! It's green as cash!

THE PROFESSOR
FALLS

Because no one is perfect enough
to love
the Professor wrestles
with the flesh.
Desire, a strong angel,
touches his thighs.
The Professor falters
but does not fall.

All the possibilities come
and stare:
The face of the Professor
floats slick as oil
on the dark waters of their eyes.
They are flawed,
too old, too much their own
to teach the melancholy secrets
of touch.
They will not practice carefully enough
the conjugation of his skin.

He is looking for a special child
with the mind of a wolf
someone has kept locked forever
in the speechless dungeon
of its own memory.
This child can be saved.
This child can be taught
his loins' tongue.

When it learns
however slowly
the rules of placing mouths together,
of fingering, of opening
to his hot understanding,

the Professor will kiss it
and fall down its eyes
into the echoing caverns
of love.

THE PERFECT
COUPLE

I thought my loneliness would never end
and rattled in this moving cage alone,
a dry seed in my sounding box of skin.

Then suddenly you came to me, my clone,
your terrifying voice to ghost my breath,
your flesh to fill the hollows in my bones.

At first I feared the way you brought me death
when you and I were juggled into place.
Now we are god. I have no other faith.

We close the other world in webs of lace.
Our cozy curtain hides us from their eyes.
We make a paradise behind our face.

Let us deny the world that we despise
and unbelieve the stars we cannot move.
We'll tell each other all the finest lies.

You are my closest neighbor. Mirror. Love.

"When the saint baptized the penguins, was this void because
the procedure of baptizing is inappropriate to be applied to
penguins, or because there is no accepted procedure of baptiz-
ing anything but humans? "
J. L. Austin,
How to Do Things With Words

On the ice beach
Sunday afternoon,
high summer
in the place the world
looks up to,
the saint lifts thin hands
like leaves transparent
but no trees grow here.
Nothing grows here.
The ground spreads gray
shades of gray
and is made of ice.
The sky ice
and the sea too ice,
and under the ice
a horizon of fish.

Everyone eats fish
here or each other:
the seals too hot
in the daylong sun,
the stern birds
punctuating summer,
the formal penguins
bowing
as they bless the saint.
His blue hands are hungry
and hot on the heads
of the penguins.
They are black,

they are white,
they are
an army of saints
with fish dreams.

Their flat feet,
their water eyes
accept his blessing
with no words.

Snow falls
at the top of your mountain,
slow soft petals, bridal white.
On the hill close to my side
there are deer whose antlers look
too heavy to hold. One is young;
it bends to look for sprouts
in your snow.

This is your print.
Miles full of trees
spread toward the distance,
their arms black against the snow.
Your house is walled by little pines,
little monks, little soldier priests
who squat in a holy circle
around your house in the sky.

No one lives in your print.
Your hands carving the wood,
your neat fingers peeling splinters away
left only the hilltop
falling into blackness
and the mountain frozen to the sky.

In my blue room
a vase of yellow flowers
stands on the green desk.
Your snow is behind them
taped like a window to the wall.
The roses are opening slowly.
Tomorrow, or on Sunday
their petals will litter my desk.
I lift the vase, touch to my lips

the cool flowers.
They are scented like women,
their petals as soft as
I think
your mouth.

OLD LOVERS
WILL NOT STAND STILL

Old lovers will not stand still
for inspection.
They waver, they feint
in your eyes.
The years between you
pile up, die and rot.
They give off an odor
as of old age and roses,
fill a river
of blood and seed
shed for someone else's sake.

Old lovers will not stand still.
The beautiful one is dumb now,
the brilliant one crazy,
the one whose smell you recognized
is brittle now as a metal insect.
Some are fading into the backgrounds
of someone else's family snapshots.
This is the falling away of hair,
like time. This is the dissolution
of memory.

You lie alone
beside the lover
you did not throw away
and visit the bodies
of all your old lovers
every night.
Their doors are closing
like the door in the surface
of water.
Their rooms are heavy with smoke
and twilight.
Though you reach

to touch them,
they will not stand still.
They waver under water
like the drowned.

THE LEAVES
ARE LOSING THE WAR

The leaves are losing the war.
They dive headfirst into the grass,
their broken wings all flaming.
The birds have mostly taken
their brief songs
and hoarded them away
but there are sparrows
still gay in their courage
and a platoon of strange geese
is waiting by the lake.
They are waiting for a signal:
for the sun to run out.

Everything is khaki:
the trees brown, the grass,
even the people are quiet now,
muffled in wool to the ears.
Under their coats
young girls' breasts are private
and the hands of the boys have forgotten
their summer yearnings.
Every morning the bus is full
of people looking away.

We make our small surrenders,
accept defeat.
Onto our shoulders the sky
drops gray stars.

THE SUN,
A HEART

There are stones within stones,
yes, and stones shooting
from stones, the halo of stones
holds us like the navel of moonlight.

There are depths in the violets,
violet fingers reach
past the violet skin
toward the sun's love.

There is, besides my brown skin,
color of soil and elemental life,
my blue skin, my red skin, my skin that reaches
without holding me in.
I touch the stone
with these skins of music
and the stones buried
in its face move.
The halo of stone
leans toward me.
I touch the violet
and it reaches.
It loves me like the sun,
like the sun, a heart, loves.

You, you here beside me,
there are beaches in your body.
Summer days we walk by the tide,
tide washes our feet.
There are mountains in you,
the skin of mountains moves
in you, a pulse.
In your smooth brown skin
is the stone skin, the stone halo,
the skin of violets and the sea.

Your halo reaches toward me,
you skin, your skins,
your body beats—
ah, the colors—
and you love me
like the sun.

FISH
POEM

Every poem
worth its salt
should have its own
fish. This
poem would cost
an ocean. It is
a fish poem.

Fish only live.
No shock can make
their eyes blink.
When they move
every action counts.
And this is grace,
this sliding.

Make my eyes fish
eyes, a pure
intelligence
without need.
Make my mouth a fish
mouth, let it know
hunger for fish.
My fish hands
on your skin,
I mouth
your fish mouth,
your fish enters me,
my breasts,
my belly
swim up
to you.

There is another
fish poem

without words.
It has gills,
it has scales,
it sings
to the water.

INSOMNIA

My mind points
in countless directions
while I toss on the gray hard water
of sleep.
I want to go traveling
down the highway
in my leg,
tumbleweed and sagebrush
and the last chance fillup station,
a smiling stranger
in a ten gallon hat
waving
as I go past,
farther and farther,
miles and miles,
toward the point
where all the lines
converge.

IN CALIFORNIA
PEOPLE DREAM

In California people dream
of flying away every night.
Nowhere special:
out of frame houses
dark as tunnels to China
they rise up happy as animals.
They follow their noses
up the moonlight,
up through the cool nights.

They fly west,
a mythical trail
past cow skulls, clothing,
tables strewn in useless heaps.
It's easy for them,
they're so tall and blond
they never needed to learn anything else.

In California people are never bored.
They write poems, smoke grass, throw pots
or sit for hours in their yards.
Winters they watch the rain all day
and when it's dark
it's summer year 'round
and they sun their perfect skins.
They can fall asleep anywhere.

GRASS
TURNED OUT GREEN

On the morning of the seventh day
God didn't plan to rest.
God was disgusted.
God looked around
and God said,
What's going on?
Things I'd planned to fly
walk, things I'd planned to swim
crawl around in the grass.
Grass turned out green,
water wet, everything's
all mixed up.

And God sat down
on a big rock
to think about
the long task of correction.
Then God saw
a shimmer on the water,
sky curdling into clouds
and all the innocent ugliness
of the world.
And God said,
Maybe that's good enough.
I'll let it be.
And God lay down and rested.
This was the seventh day.

This is our seventh year together.
Our plans are mouse tracks in a field of snow.
Shadows circle like owls around us and the fox is near.
We lie in the grass,
embrace each other's weakness,
have one thing God forgot:
someone to rest with
and to blame.

THE SOURCE
OF THE SINGING

Under everything, everything
a movement, slow as hair growth,
as the subtle click of cells turning
into other cells, the life in us
that grows as mountains grow.
Under everything this movement,
stars and wind circle around the smaller
circles of the grass, and the birds caged
in the kitchen sing it over and over,
inexplicably in their sweet chirps.

I feel it sometimes like today
somewhere in my torso, perhaps
sweet in the belly; this must be
what carrying a child is like.
I sit at a table and feel something
move with the pain of just before tears.
What is it the body says to me,
these tender aches that make me glad?
Not even one syllable is clear,
but if you were near I would tell you,
and you might lay your hand where the talking
starts and the pain, where my life
is still moving like an eaten live thing
and push your warmth into mine,
here, into the source of the singing.